GOLFING TOUGH

Three Simple Methods to Improve Your Performance Under Pressure

> Note: As an authorized purchaser of Playing Tough, you may download Dr. J. C. McCroskey's Relaxation audio in MP3 format from http://www.roberthstrickland.com/Relaxation/Relaxation.htm. (Case Sensitive) Click "Download the relaxation audio here." When prompted, type the User Name: "purchaser" and the Password: "authorized."

Powers and Strickland

GOLFING TOUGH

By

Will Powers and Bob Strickland

Edited by: Lois Powers, Sue Strickland

Illustrated by: Bob and Sue Strickland

Published by:

Robert H Strickland Associates LLC

P. O. Box 1388

Everett, Washington 98206-1388 USA

Phone/Fax: 425-258-6796

All rights reserved. No part of this book may be reproduced or transmitted in any form or by any means, electronic or mechanical, including photocopying, recording, or by any information storage and retrieval system without written permission from the authors, except for the inclusion of brief quotations in a review.

Copyright 2016 by William G. Powers and Robert H. Strickland

Library of Congress Control Number: 2016907517

Powers, William G. 1943, and Strickland, Robert H., 1944

Golfing Tough / by Will Powers and Bob Strickland

p. 94 cm.

Includes index.

ISBN 978-0-9635919-3-7

Dedication

Will and Lois Powers

"We dedicate our contribution to this book to our mothers (Mary T. Marquis and Frances M. Peterson). The foundation of our lives was strong and built upon the highest of values. We thank each parent for their strength and support during the entire course of our lives."

Bob and Sue Strickland

"We dedicate our contribution to the thousands of avid golfers who try to be as skilled as their time and physical capabilities allow. Also, we wish to recognize the efforts of the many instructors and coaches that spend countless hours pondering the mysteries of golf for no reasons other than to help others play just a little bit better. Among these, we include the late Richie Porter of Top Shelf Golf, whose impressive athletic ability and concern for others led him into golf instruction. Stricken with severe arthritis, he was not able to continue in the game that he loved, and he left us unexpectedly at the young age of 37."

Acknowledgements

This book has been a family project from the very beginning. Each of us acknowledge the support, sensitive editing, and integration of specialized knowledge from each of the four contributors (Will/Lois and Bob/Sue). Without each other, this project would never have been completed.

From Will Powers: Special thanks go to Bruce McDonald, Dr. James C. McCroskey and Dr. H. Wayland Cummings for delivering appropriate "motivational stimulation" at various points in my life development which ultimately led to my ability to contribute to this project.

From Bob Strickland: Thanks go to my long-time friend, Tom Pfeil, president of MEDALT, a training media firm, for his advice regarding the utility and continuity of this book. An expert in the field of instructional design, Tom is also a highly-skilled golfer and bowler with many years of experience and achievement in the sports. With a keen mind to go with his impressive background, Tom was able to make a unique contribution.

The authors acknowledge the following organization for providing some of the images used in this book:

"Presentation Task Force" - New Vision Technologies, Incorporated, 38 Auriga Drive, Unit 13, Nepean, Ontario Canada, K2E 8A5, Telephone: 613-727-8184. Copyrighted, All Rights Reserved.

Forward

Every day of a tournament is filled with potential high-pressure or clutch situations. Golfers who perform well in the clutch, Golf Tough.

Golfers who perform well under pressure are admired because this ability is rare. They "stay in there", getting the ball as close to the cup as they can. They are "locked in" mentally, all of the time.

People who fail to play well under pressure simply don't know how to establish a successful Golfing Tough mentality.

To be successful under pressure, you need to know:
- How you – yourself – create your own clutch situations
- What happens to your body in clutch situations
- Methods to ensure high-quality performance under pressure
- How to make these methods automatic through practice
- How to use these methods in all forms of competition

We want you to be a success by learning how to:
- Make personal "success decisions"
- Relax under pressure
- Increase your self-confidence
- Practice success on and off the course
- Make a "mental routine" work for you

Golfing Tough shows you how to use a few simple, proven mental skills to put you in control of what you want to accomplish. If you use these methods faithfully, you will eagerly take on responsibility for your own performance. You will be a master of your own success.

These methods will make you a problem-solver. You will stop blaming yourself, your equipment, course conditions, or even other persons for your failures. You will understand that no one is successful all of the time. Failure will become just another opportunity to seek solutions and perform better the next time.

Even if you master only one method and use it consistently, you should see a dramatic increase in your performance potential under conditions that are extremely stressful for others. At the very least, you will get greater enjoyment and less frustration from golf.

Use the encouraging "Keys" throughout this book to help you remember what to do. Let's begin now, so you can start using these mental skills with your own physical game right away! Here is your first key.

 Work hard, be persistent, learn the strategies, and review the keys often. Success in competition will become much easier for you. You will Golf Tough!

Like everything else that is worthwhile and rare, Golfing Tough does not come without belief, change, dedication, and practice. The only real question you must answer is "Do I really want to improve my golfing performance?" If you answer "Yes!", it's just a question of "want to" and "know how to!"

Disclaimer

The techniques described herein, like those recommended by others, may not be effective for all persons. Therefore, the authors/publisher disclaim any responsibility and liability in connection with any actions taken or not taken based on the content of this book.

Will Powers, Ph. D., Lewisville, Texas
Bob Strickland, M. S., Everett, Washington

Contents

Dedication 5

Acknowledgements 7

Forward 9
    Disclaimer 10

1   You Can Golf Tough! 13
    Clutch Situations 13
    How Does a Clutch Situation Develop? 15
    The Ultimate Clutch Solution: Your Mind 20
    Mental Control and the Physical Game 21

2   You Can Consciously Choose to Be a Success! 23
    Non-conscious Decision # 1: To Get Anxious or Stressed-out 24
    Non-conscious Decision # 2: To Fear Failure 25
    Non-conscious Decision # 3: To Fear Success 26
    Non-conscious Decision # 4: To Believe That You Will Fail 27
    Non-conscious Decision # 5: To Believe That It Just Doesn't Matter 28
    Non-conscious Decision # 6: To Tense Up and Try Harder 29
    Non-conscious Decision # 7: To Become Distracted 30
    Non-conscious Decision # 8: To Practice Only the Physical Game 31
    Conscious Decisions: The Hidden Success Options 32

3   You Can Build Self-confidence! 35
    Taking Control of Yourself 35
    Self-talk and Behavior Drills 39

4   You Can Use the Super Powers of Your Mind! 47
    Visualizing Your Way to Success 47
    Mental Practice Drills 52

5   You Can Relax, Anywhere, Anytime! 61
    Using Willful Relaxation 61

	Relaxation Drills	66
6	You Can Make Mental Toughness Routine!	71
	Taking Control of Your Mental Environment	71
	Mental Toughness Routine	72
	MTR Incorporation Drill	75
	A Final Word	77
Appendix A	Building a Reliable Physical Game	79
	Classic Golf Instruction, (Brent Kelly, About Sports)	79
	Modern Books	80
Appendix B	Making a Relaxation Tape or CD	81
	Directions for Making a Relaxation Tape or CD	81
Appendix C	Making a Coping Tape or CD	85
	Directions for Making a Coping Tape or CD	85
	Directions for Making a Booster (Relaxation/Coping) Tape or CD	88

1 You Can Golf Tough!

Golfing Tough is successfully meeting the mental challenge of performing well, regardless of the level of competition or the amount of pressure the golfer is experiencing. It is easiest to see if someone is Golfing Tough when the pressure level is high, often called a "clutch" situation. **Clutch situations are common in golf because golfers come under pressure fairly often.**

Clutch Situations

People "in the clutch" definitely place themselves under pressure, stress, and tension simply because they have an extremely high desire to succeed. A clutch situation develops when someone experiences an unusually strong emotional reaction related to achieving one or more important goals (like needing a birdie or a par to win the match).

We never forget those special moments in golf when we desire success more than anything else. Almost every golfer, regardless of handicap, can tell you about one instance in which he or she has met the challenge of performing well in a clutch situation — Golfing Tough. Those times when we have achieved our goals stand out in our minds, especially if such successes are few and far between.

Of course, most of us also vividly remember those instances when we did not perform well under pressure. Although we put those negative memories in the backs of our minds, they are still there and active. These negatives create a very clear history the next time we are in a similar situation. Then, the history in our minds tends to repeat itself.

Because we focus so much upon the potential for failure, we do not perform well in the clutch. Unfortunately, we often create unreasonable expectations of ourselves. We think we should be perfect and succeed all of the time. And when we do not meet these expectations, we tend to feel that we are failures.

 **Take a really good look at what you expect from yourself and then ask, "Are my expectations reasonable?"**

After all is said and done, few professional golfers ever perform at their true potential in clutch situations. The ones who do, cannot do it 100% of the time. You can see this for yourself on televised matches. If the professionals have difficulty in performing in the clutch, is it reasonable for you to expect a superior level of performance from yourself — all of the time? Probably not! In fact, if at your best you succeed 80% of the time, then under high-pressure golfing conditions, your most reasonable expectation would be that you will succeed 80% of the time. If a particular instance happens to be one of the 80%, then that is super! If it happens to be one of the 20%, then that is too bad. Be reasonable with yourself; dwelling on "failure" because of unreasonable expectations is absolutely foolish!

If you have reasonable expectations, you still may not perform as well in the clutch as you would like, simply due to a lack of know-how and practice. But, you can perform up to your potential if you put as much hard work into your mental game as you do into your physical game. The mental game is actually quite simple — it is common sense.

Every golfer practices the physical game. Few actually practice their mental games. But consistent winners have their mental acts together. They practice and use mental skills consistently even though they may not be aware that these skills are being used. Therefore, they perform well under pressure!

The consistent and effective mental control of a refined physical game distinguishes real long-term winners from the rest of the field.

 **You can practice mental and physical skills at the same time!**

We show you how you can practice physical and mental skills at the same time. Learn and practice the methods of mental control and put them into your game plan — all of the time. You will have more frequent success under pressure.

How Does a Clutch Situation Develop?

At any time in any kind of competitive environment, you can become involved in a clutch situation. For example, a competitive round may begin with very little pressure on you or your opponent. As the round progresses, pressure increases on both of you, especially if your scores are close and the winner's prize is valuable. The pressure may reach such a high level that a clutch situation develops for one or both of you. The golfer who "golfs tough" will win more frequently.

As we said before, a "clutch situation" develops when you experience an unusually strong emotional reaction related to achieving one or more important goals. Some examples of potential clutch situations are:

- Needing to make a birdie to win
- Needing to make a difficult putt to win
- Needing a subtle shot out of a sand trap
- Needing to clear a large water hazard
- Needing to hit correctly out of tall grass
- Needing a good shot immediately after making a bad shot
- Needing to hit while standing on an uneven surface

Clutch situations are very personal. A clutch situation to one person may not produce stress or tension in another. You make your own!

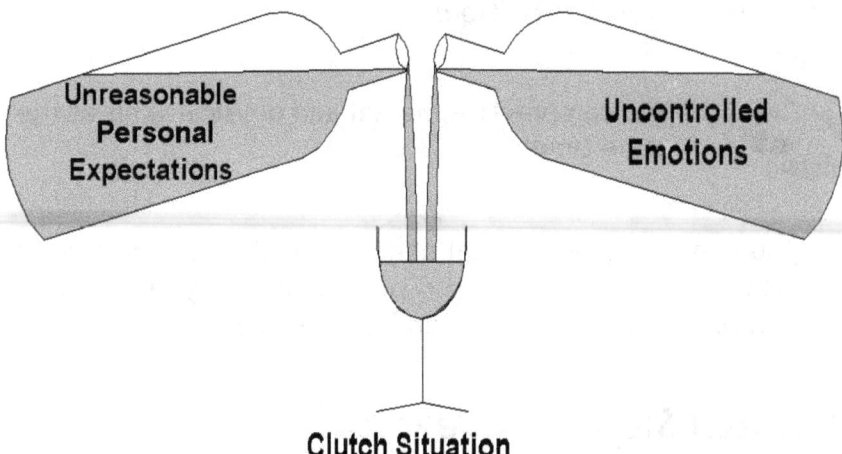

Clutch Situation

Each person makes his/her own personal clutch situations! This is a result of two basic problems: (1) unreasonable personal expectations and (2) uncontrolled emotions. We call these "clutch problems", and we would like you to understand them. Keep in mind that every performer experiences one or more of these problems at some time in his or her development, but those who Golf Tough under pressure have learned to solve these problems.

Clutch Problem #1: Trying To Achieve Unreasonable Goals

A goal is a specific idea of what you wish to achieve – an expectation. Successful performance in any clutch situation in golfing involves the achievement of three goals: (1) the performance – the quality of the swing and shot, (2) the outcome – getting a birdie, and (3) the prize – to win.

1. **The first level goal, the performance of a high-quality shot, is the only goal that is basically under your complete control.** It is the foundation achievement that actually allows you an opportunity to reach the second level, or intermediate, goal.

2. **The second level goal, the outcome of getting the ball in the cup within par or less than par, is not completely under your control.** You may get a bad bounce on a very well-executed shot, for example. "Good golfers do not make birdies! They make shots. Golf balls make birdies!"

   Performance is the important goal. The frequency of birdies as well as the frequency of winning will rise naturally as accuracy and consistency of performance improve.

3. **The third level goal, the reward or prize of winning the match or tournament is called the outcome. It is never under your direct control.** Anything that is not under your direct control should not even enter your mind. You should ignore it at all times, or you will allow it to interfere with your performance.

Focus on the goal that is within your immediate reaching distance. Do not focus upon goals that are not under your direct control.

Having lofty ambitions is wonderful! There is absolutely nothing wrong with your dreaming of being the professional golfing "Rookie of the Year", for example. But, if you focus upon that high-level goal instead of the most immediate and reachable goal of a perfectly-executed shot, you may never reach the higher one. You can maintain consistent success results and reach great heights if you place easier goals as "stepping stones" in front of you on the way to more difficult ones.

> **Example:** You must execute well (Goal 1) before you can birdie consistently (Goal 2). You must birdie consistently before you can win consistently (Goal 3). You cannot bypass Goal 1! But, if you achieve Goal 1, you will achieve Goal 2, and possibly, Goal 3.

If you allow even a small bit of your focus on Goal 1 (execution) to drift to Goal 2 (scoring) or Goal 3 (winning), you lower your potential to execute. You corrupt your ability to make the physical movements that allow good shots and winning!

The first major contribution to your performance success in clutch situations is to focus only upon that immediate goal under your direct control. Place your complete mental concentration only on the goal of perfect execution, one shot at a time!

Clutch Problem #2: Letting Your Emotions Get Out Of Control.

Emotions can be pleasurable when falling in love. But, they are often troublesome when trying to perform in high-stress situations. Negative emotions destroy positive potential.

Think about the times when you practiced golf while angry. You would slam the club face down on the ground or fling the club. When you were depressed, you would give up and make a shot without any attention. This illustrates that you cannot practice productively when you are upset or emotional.

On the other hand, positive emotions promote positive potential. When you experience positive emotions, you carefully choose an isolated and relaxed setting for practice. You use practice to develop and refine muscle habits associated with a high-quality swing and shot. Some of your finest golfing (performing) is done during practice under conditions of positive emotion. You repeat effective movements over and over in a relaxed condition; you concentrate!

The second major contribution to your performance success in clutch situations is to create the same mental environment in both competition and practice. Create the same emotions during competition that you create during practice.

A few golfers can do this by making practice like competition. But for most golfers, the key to their success is making competition more like practice. This definitely does not mean that practice is play time and competition becomes just a time to play. It means that the mental approach you use in practice should be the same one you use during all competition.

The Ultimate Clutch Problem: What Happens to Your Body in a Clutch Situation?

What is the major emotional difference between a practice environment and a competitive environment? It is the presence of a prize for winning or a penalty for losing! During competition, your desire to achieve important goals (good execution or winning) combines with your fear of possible failure, causing negative emotions to rise within you. Clutch situations impact your body's ability to perform at a consistently high level.

In the heat of competition, with a significant outcome (winning or losing), most golfers will eventually focus on winning, allowing their attention to stray from the all-important performance. This is exactly why so many golfers are not winners! If you fall into this trap, you become emotionally and physically stressed. You become "emotional." Your muscles become tense and your movements erratic. You lose the fine physical edge you developed during practice. Realizing that you have lost the "feel" of reliable movements, you become even more emotional, and your performance suffers even more.

We humans are strange critters. When our minds are relaxed, our bodies are relaxed. When our minds are up-tight, our bodies get up-tight. An unemotional robot is an excellent mental model. But, because humans can never hope to achieve a robot's lack of emotion, we have to do what is necessary to wipe out the negative emotions that interfere with our performance under stressful conditions.

You can have emotional control! Just begin a systematic plan for developing, practicing, and using mental skills during practice and competition.

> **Example:** Assume that you really, really want to get a birdie so your team can win. However, you know that you haven't been swinging well lately and fear that you will not birdie now.

These negative thoughts and emotions interfere with the ability of your muscles to perform at the relaxed skill level you achieve during practice. The anticipation of failing to reach the second level goal (making the birdie) causes nervousness (anxiety) that keeps your muscles from executing the movements with peak accuracy and consistency (your first level goal).

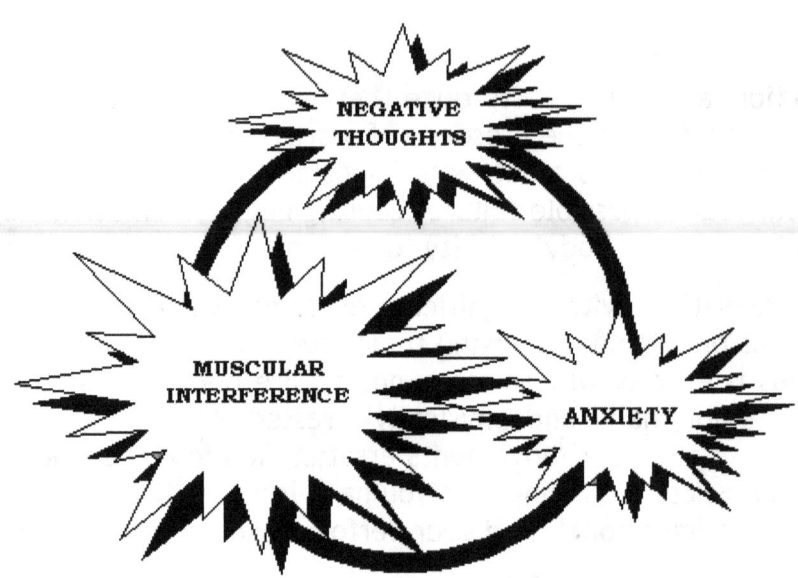

Anxiety and a smooth shot cannot go hand-in-hand. Anxiety represents an obstacle that we must overcome to reach our goals successfully.

The Ultimate Clutch Solution: Your Mind

Your thoughts are your reality — regardless of what is actually happening. Therefore, any situation that you believe is "clutch" is indeed clutch — to you.

Your thoughts about your situation, your ability to perform, and the importance of your goals produce the framework within which your body has to make accurate and consistent movements. The situation is alive; you cannot be neutral. You always react in some way to the situation. Your key to success is to get your mind working for you — not against you.

 You can willfully change how you think and act.

Those situations that are "bad" can become "not so bad" after all. You have a miraculous ability to bring about change. Just make a choice to think and act differently. Your success or failure is under your control through what you choose to believe; it is truly up to you! As you become more successful in clutch situations, your confidence will grow, opening the door to future success.

Later, we show you how to restructure your thoughts to produce a reasonable reality, allowing you to perform at your maximum talent level. However, at this point, it is important to consider some points about the physical game of golf.

Mental Control and the Physical Game

If you have a poor physical game, you must improve it so it will not be a stumbling block to your progress in using mental skills. While it is true that there are many ways a golfer can propel the ball down the fairway and achieve good scores, some golfing forms are structurally unsound and do not allow consistency.

 **Consistency of physical movement is vital to the development of a strong mental game.**

You must be able to trust your movements to produce the same results every time. Otherwise, it will be impossible to build confidence, no matter how well you apply the mental skills explained in this book! If you have a sound, consistent physical game, mental skills are of tremendous benefit to you! To help you with your physical game, we offer the following guidelines.

1. Make sure that your clubs are of appropriate lengths and the grips are of a correct fit to allow you good control on each and every shot. You may not be aware of unproductive movements, but they will prevent you from developing the proper mental focus and building confidence.

2. Establish an ongoing relationship with an instructor or coach who understands the physical game, who is a skilled observer and teacher, and who will help you attain your goals.

3. Make sure that each and every overall shot is decisive. Strive to be stable (sure-footed). Keep your form economical, without any unnecessary movements. In fact, if you cannot think of a logical reason to perform a certain movement, eliminate it!

4. Develop your physical game around the logical. Think through everything you hear, discussing it with your instructor, ensuring that you understand why you make your own collection of movements and behaviors. Everything you do must have a valid reason.

   See Appendix A Building a Reliable Physical Game for a list of excellent golf instructional books.

The following chapters describe three different ways to improve your potential to perform well under stressful conditions. One or more of these methods will work for you. You may find that all three methods will work together to give you the best results, performing as well as you are physically capable of under pressure.

 **You are in control! Consciously choose what you want to focus your thoughts on. Golfing Tough is simple and easy. It takes a bit of practice but once you've mastered the basics, Golfing Tough becomes second nature.**

2 You Can Consciously Choose to Be a Success!

We frequently do not think about how we will react in many situations, even when our reactions may be important to our personal success potential! Rather, we develop non-conscious habits, reacting to whatever happens without thinking about it. These habits control our lives; for example, do you still think about how to tie your shoes?

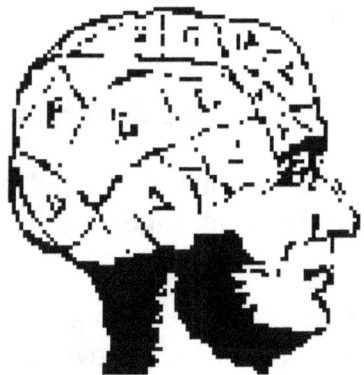

Because we react without thinking about the circumstances, many of our decisions are non-conscious. With non-conscious decisions, the potential to make errors — to react inappropriately in any given situation — is very high. There are many such non-conscious decisions that produce error and increase the potential for failure.

 **Non-conscious decisions are always poor decisions. They are like letting your worst enemy make your decisions for you!**

In this chapter, we explain many non-conscious decisions that keep golfers and other athletes from performing at their full potential. Potentially good golfers who perform poorly in competition have made one or more of the following non-conscious decisions for themselves!

- To get anxious or stressed out
- To fear failure
- To fear success
- To believe that they will fail
- To believe that it just doesn't matter
- To tense up and try harder
- To become distracted
- To practice only the physical game

To avoid the destructive effect that such non-conscious decisions have on your game, you need to understand what these decisions mean and what tough golfers do to overcome them. Let's look at them one-by-one.

Non-conscious Decision # 1: To Get Anxious or Stressed-out

If you are mentally anxious or stressed-out during competition, you will be physically up-tight and unable to perform with the smoothness and consistency that you have in practice.

Tough golfers are not immune to stress. They just deal with it effectively. Because they know that anxiety or stress is a natural part of high-level competition, they simply meet it head-on and control their reactions to it.

They have a plan that involves using exactly the methods explained in this book. They use mental skills to overcome stress.

 **Meet stress head-on and take control!**

Non-conscious Decision # 2: To Fear Failure

Some people fear failure, but no one can reasonably expect to be successful all of the time. It's that simple. A major difference between people who perform well in the clutch and those who don't is how reasonable their self-expectations are.

Tough golfers know that they hit the ball very well — 80% of the time, for example. They may also know that if they hit the ball well, they will reach the secondary goal of making a birdie. Of course, some of the time they will fail to birdie because of a poor shot, misalignment, or an unlucky break.

Because tough golfers know these odds, they do not fear failure. They are more reasonable about the demands they make on themselves. They concentrate on achieving only that which is in their control — a high-quality shot. If they happen to make one of the 20 poor shots out of 100 that do not have a good result, it's unfortunate but not devastating. They know that they can reasonably expect to be successful 80 times out of 100.

 **Mentally, the tough golfers focus on the rate of success — not the rate of failure. They know that over the long haul, the odds are with them, not against them.**

Non-conscious Decision # 3: To Fear Success

Although difficult to believe, some people actually decide to fear being successful! They think that if they become too successful then everyone will expect success from them all of the time. Because they know that they cannot be successful all of the time, it presents an assured failure situation.

So, in a backwards sort of way, the fear of ultimate failure produces a fear of immediate success that produces the anxiety that guarantees the body will not perform well in clutch situations. As this long, complicated reasoning occurs, it obviously creates an environment of failure.

Tough golfers know that no one expects them to be successful all of the time. They do not expect the same of themselves either! They know that, if they set their sights on goals that they can achieve, bigger successes will follow. They do not fear success because they are successful in reaching realistic goals all of the time.

 **Tough golfers do not expect to be successful all of the time.**

Non-conscious Decision # 4: To Believe That You Will Fail

Some golfers remain "hung up" on the times that they have failed (the 20% factor). As they find themselves in a clutch situation, they remind themselves that, because they haven't performed well in the past, they will not perform well in the present situation. Remember how the body believes the mind? If you believe you are going to fail, the odds are the body will make every effort for these thoughts to come true.

Tough golfers are aware of the times when they failed — but only for a short time. They simply "go back to the drawing board" and work out a winning strategy.

Failure drops from their minds as they work productively on their physical and mental games in anticipation of the next competition.

 **Tough golfers go back to the drawing board. Failure drops from their minds.**

Non-conscious Decision # 5: To Believe That It Just Doesn't Matter

Once again, the mind dictates to the body. If you convince yourself that it doesn't really matter whether you execute well, the body believes you and doesn't bother to execute well. It becomes a self-fulfilling prophecy.

Tough golfers get a good feeling from a well-executed shot. To them, the proper feel and anticipation of the birdie or the par is often more confidence-boosting than the birdie or par itself. They are performance-oriented. They "get a kick" out of a well struck ball — both in practice and in competition. To them, every shot matters!

 **Tough golfers get a kick out of a well-struck ball.**

Non-conscious Decision # 6: To Tense Up and Try Harder

In sports such as football or boxing, success depends upon explosive force and tremendous exertion of muscle. Golf is very different. Success is dependent upon smooth execution created by the proper balance between relaxation and tension. As soon as you try to "give it everything you've got," your muscular balance goes out of whack — and so does your ability to execute well.

It is easy to spot a golfer who tenses up under pressure. Somewhere, the tense golfer has heard that "trying harder" involves squeezing the club with both hands, and digging in too much, and using excessive waggle during the setup.

During the shot, this golfer may lean over, take too wide a stance, jerk the club up into a clipped-off swing, and follow through with extraordinary vigor! If the golfer is particularly "keyed up", he may follow a poor shot with a dramatic curse and a swift pounding of his club in the grass. **An up-tight golfer may fly off the handle.**

Tough golfers are also tempted to physically overpower a stressful situation! But they do not give in to temptation. They systematically take their setups, calm their minds and bodies, focus, and make unhurried, high-quality swings. This is Golfing Tough under pressure.

 **Tough golfers systematically calm themselves, focus, and confidently strike the ball.**

Non-conscious Decision # 7: To Become Distracted

When you are distracted, it means that you have made an unconscious decision not to concentrate. Golfing requires complete concentration and internal focus. When your mind is busy looking outside the shot and execution factors, it is not sufficiently focused.

A lack of concentration on the immediate task of a high-quality shot opens the door to "seeing" extraneous movement or "hearing" noises that are typically easy to "shut out", but which are now allowed to become disruptive.

Tough golfers are so focused that they would not even notice "fans" lined up on both sides screaming, yelling, and waving their arms. Proper mental focus is a simple decision to make — not a hard one. Just like the physical game, the mental game takes practice to achieve.

 **Tough golfers concentrate and stay focused.**

Non-conscious Decision # 8: To Practice Only the Physical Game

Many golfers feel that all they have to do to improve clutch performance is practice more and practice harder. This is not practicing smart!

Don't get us wrong. Practicing the physical game is important for developing and refining physical skills. If you have a mechanically poor shot, you cannot control it physically or mentally! But merely practicing more or harder will do absolutely nothing for the mental game that becomes so critical for success under clutch conditions.

To perform at maximum physical potential in clutch situations you have to learn the rules of the mental game and practice, practice, practice the mental skills.

Practice the Mental Game as You Would the Physical Game

Tough golfers practice their mental games right along with their physical games. Much of their golfing is done during competition, therefore, they use mental skills more frequently than recreational golfers. But, the point is that they know mental skills and use them all of the time. They do not play without a purpose. They do not mindlessly hit balls. They use their minds to create consistently good shots.

Your battle plan for success involves forcing negative, non-conscious decisions up to the conscious level. Then, make positive conscious decisions about your reactions to situations. These decisions determine your success or failure potential and deserve your best, thoughtful efforts; they involve you!

Unless you consciously recognize your negative non-conscious decisions and change them, they will usually stay in your non-conscious level of awareness. Just like a law, they will stay in force! They will continue to interfere with your performance and lower your confidence.

Conscious Decisions: The Hidden Success Options

Your approach to consistent high-quality performance under stress begins with consciously selecting the following options that work best for you! All of the options covered in this book work; the question you must answer is, "Which options work best to make me comfortable in the situations where I need help?"

Therefore, here is a list of the following chapters that describe the basic success options in detail; you should choose from these. "Seriously try" each and every one of the options exactly in the manner we describe. Then, follow the lead of many golfers and other athletes and incorporate into your performance system all of the options that make sense to you, that fit your personality, and allow you to reach your goals.

You will be able to achieve the goals listed under each chapter heading, below.

Chapter 3 You Can Build Self-confidence!
- Increase your confidence through what you say to yourself and others.
- Establish the correct frame of mind for success.
- Act like a success.

Chapter 4 You Can Use the Super Powers of Your Mind!
- Visualize successful performance.
- Practice anytime, anywhere.
- Focus your mind for consistent, successful performance.

Chapter 5 You Can Relax, Anywhere, Anytime!
- Relax physically and mentally.
- Set and achieve realistic goals for yourself.
- Increase your knowledge of yourself and how you really feel about and react to real situations.

Chapter 6 You Can Make Mental Toughness Routine!
- Organize your thoughts and actions for consistent, high-level performance in practice and in tournaments.

It is easy and simple to perform well under both regular and special conditions. All it takes is useful knowledge and practice, practice, practice!

 **You can have a calmer, more systematic approach to golf, especially during competition. You can Golf Tough; and others will marvel at your skill in the clutch, never even realizing what you are doing.**

You Can Consciously Choose to Be a Success!

3 You Can Build Self-confidence!

The relationship between the mind and body is amazing. Your body simply cannot tell the difference between reality and your imagination. What the mind tells the body to believe, the body believes.

> **Example: Do you know of anyone who had a nightmare and woke up sweating, screaming and flailing about? Even though the nightmare was only imagined, the mind convinced the body it was actually happening, and the body reacted.**

Taking Control of Yourself

The following sections describe the concepts of thoughts, conversation, and behavior. See the **Self-talk and Behavior Drills** section for detailed directions.

Thoughts (Self-talk)

Thoughts are a form of programming, or "talking to" your brain. The key to success or failure in golf and other sporting events is programming the mind. If you program your mind to tell the body it will fail, then the body will fail. However, if you program the mind to tell the body it will succeed, then the body will succeed. The secret to all of this is that the mind has to believe the scenario you present. If the mind believes, the body believes. Thinking positive gives your muscles the best chance for a high-quality performance.

 **Destructive Self-talk Off — Productive Self-talk On!**

The extent to which your mind believes you will be successful is directly related to what you tell it to believe. So, you have to start by exploring what you tell yourself about yourself. If this self-talk is not productive, then all you have to do is replace destructive thoughts with productive self-talk. It's easy!

Talking With Others

Another form of programming your brain is the actual talk you have with others about your potential to succeed. So often, we hear many golfers predicting failure for themselves. "No way can I make this par!", or "I am not very good at the short game." Most of the time, they are good fortune tellers because their brains hear this talk and believe that it should produce a failure event.

 **Say positive things; do not say negative things!**

The real trick is to say positive things to get the odds in your favor. Some positive statements are, "I will land the ball within five feet of the cup.", or "I will strike the ball squarely on the next shot." Obviously, simply talking positively will not automatically produce success for you every time. But, getting the odds in your favor will have an undeniable impact on your performance.

Behavior

Any action you take that disrupts a positive mental attitude puts the odds against your success. When frustrated, some golfers commonly engage in disruptive behavior, such as:

- Yelling or making obscene gestures
- Cursing
- Kicking the ground or equipment
- Stomping around other players in the area
- Purposely acting disgusted

All of these actions detract from the positive mental focus needed for high-quality execution on the next shot.

Contrary to what many people think, being a jerk does not "release" your frustrations and allow you to concentrate on your next shot. Instead, such behaviors form part of your mental history and serve as a reality check for the brain. In other words, these types of behaviors confirm that you are expecting failure. With all of this mental energy focused on failure, it is not surprising that successful performance in the clutch is a rare event.

The most productive action you can take involves knowing the difference between what is in your control and what is not in your control. Making birdies is simply not a sure thing. It is not constantly under your control.

 Frustration over conditions not under your control is a total waste of mental energy. Focus only on that which is under your control — the high-quality execution of your shot.

Recognizing Negatives

Negative thoughts, talk, and behavior often originate from a non-conscious level. Therefore, they can be very difficult to recognize. Yet, if you cannot identify what you are thinking, saying, and doing, you cannot correct the situation and improve our success potential.

 Self-awareness is the first step to progress! Listen to yourself.

You Can Build Self-confidence!

Replacing Negatives with Positives

Once you know how to recognize negatives, what should you do about them? The answer is to replace them with positives!

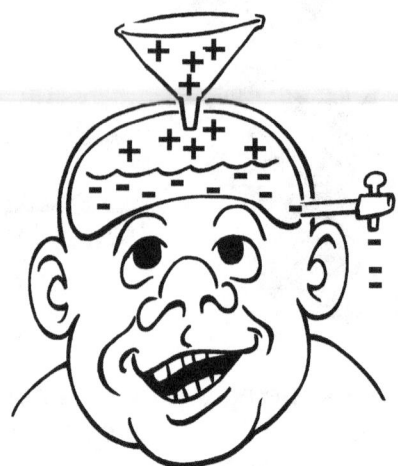

Do not emphasize "getting rid" of bad habits. To do so may result in keeping them. Rather, emphasize substituting good habits for bad ones. This is a more productive and successful approach.

 Substitute good, positive habits for bad, negative ones.

Practicing Positive Thinking, Talking, and Behaving

Once you know positive things to think, to say, and to do, it is your responsibility to enact them at all times. Even though you may be enthusiastic at first, it still may be a little difficult to catch yourself applying negatives. However, you may be able to get a little help from your playing partners. Tell them what you are trying to accomplish. Be honest! Ask them to let you know every time you slip up and move toward negative talk or behavior. Make it fun for them to tell you or they won't help you. Volunteer to contribute to your playing partners every time they catch you.

In a very short time, you will be able to change your perspective and enhance your ability to perform effectively under the worst conditions. This joint helping project will also contribute to cohesiveness and spirit.

 **Be a success by thinking like a success, talking like a success, and acting like a success.**

Self-talk and Behavior Drills

For the drills on the following pages, keep a notebook so you can see your total progress. Label a page or section with the name of the drill at the top. Your notes are private, so keep them in your bag between shots.

Recognizing Negatives

This drill is designed to help you recognize negative thoughts, talk, and behavior that you may not be aware of. Follow the directions below; think hard, and be honest with yourself! Self-awareness is the first step toward progress!

Directions

In the space below, write a list of negative thoughts, talk, and behavior that you remember doing. Make these items specific and list as many as you want; use your notebook or a separate sheet of paper if necessary. Then, show the list to friends and ask them to add anything they have noticed that is not on your list.

> **Example:** "I kick the ground whenever I am angry." or "When I do not drive well on my first shot, I loaf on the second shot." or "I curse when I miss a putt."

a. _____

b. _____

c. _____

d. _____

e. _____

Replacing Negatives with Positives

This drill is an extension of the previous one. **Once you know what your negative thoughts, talk, and behavior are, you need to replace them with positives.** If you do not replace them, other negatives will take the place of the ones that you have abandoned. Nature hates a void! It is better to decide for yourself what to replace abandoned negatives with. Follow the directions below; think hard, and be honest with yourself!

Directions

Now, write a list of positive thoughts, talk and behavior that you would like to replace those on the "neagtives" list. Be specific. Be reasonable.

> **Example:** "When I am angry, I take a deep breath and relax.", or "When I do not make a birdie, I welcome the opportunity to par as a chance to practice good shot-making."

a. _____

b. _____

c. _____

d. _____

e. _____

You Can Build Self-confidence!

Practicing Self-Talk at Home or When Alone

Take control of your thoughts. Use your "quiet time" to eliminate negative self-statements by replacing them with positive, reasonable statements about yourself. Examine your own self-talk by "thinking out loud", talking rather than merely thinking the thoughts. You will be surprised to learn how much you put yourself down when it is completely undeserved.

1. Take at least 15 minutes each day in private to evaluate yourself — your intelligence, your skill, your talent, your physical appearance. Talk to yourself out loud, noting what you say is positive or negative.
2. When you hear yourself say something that is unreasonable or negative, immediately replace the statement with something reasonable and positive. Soon, you will be thinking of yourself fairly, in realistic and positive terms.

Summary
1. Make a statement about yourself.
2. Evaluate if negative (unreasonable) or positive (reasonable).
3. Replace negative with positive.
4. Record results and evaluate your progress

Recording Results

Using the following headings, make notations in your notebook.

Date	Quoted Statement + or -	Replacing (Positive) Statement
1/30	I can't drive straight.	I drive as straight as anyone.

Copy down every self-statement, no matter how unusual. You must rate the statement as either positive or negative. Replace all negative statements with positive ones; write these replacing statements down also. When you have entered all statements for a 15-minute session, draw a heavy line under the last entry to indicate when the session ended.

Evaluating Progress

Look at each "block" of statements closely. As you are seriously pursuing your goal, positive "Quoted Statements" will become more frequent than negative ones.

 **Negative statements and thoughts disappear as you work diligently toward your goal.**

Practicing Positive Self-Talk During Solo Physical Practice

Improve your performance through the influence of positive self statements. Force yourself to think — and act — positively when you practice until it becomes automatic.

1. Practice the physical game, making sure that you are lined up properly for each shot and that you are executing correctly.
2. Then, make at least 60 practice shots for positive self-talk practice. Before each shot, make a positive statement to yourself right before you start movement from your setup. Make the same positive statement to yourself immediately after you hit your ball.

Summary

1. Make positive statement about yourself.
2. Execute properly.
3. Repeat positive statement to yourself.
4. Record results.
5. Evaluate your progress

Recording Results

Keep a numerical score on a regulation scorecard. Although you do not have to write down the actual statement you made (you may, if you like), simply place a check mark in the hole box somewhere to show that you made the positive statement before and after each shot. You may allow a practice partner (or a trusted caddie) to record results and evaluate you. Simply make the positive statement before and after each shot to your practice partner, and ask him or her to check off the hole for you and, if desired, write your statements and his observations in your notebook.

Evaluating Progress

Look back at any notes you may have, correlating with the scorecard and paying attention to any indications that you may be performing better when you use the positive self-statements.

 Keep trying; it may take a few weeks of steady practice before you notice a significant change.

Practicing Self-Talk with Partner Intervention

Help yourself and your practice partner(s) eliminate all negative self-statements by replacing them with positive, reasonable statements.

1. Agree with your practice partner(s) to take a portion of practice (1 hour, for example) to evaluate your "thinking out loud" while practice golfing.
2. While you are being evaluated, your partner should stop you whenever you say something negative and make you restate the item in a positive, constructive manner. Remember that positive words may be positive can be stated in a negative tone of voice, making the statement a hidden negative.
   - If you stop thinking out loud, your partner should prompt you by saying, "What are you thinking?"
   - If you respond with a negative statement, your partner should redirect you.
   - If your response is positive, then you are making progress on your own!
3. Be sure to reciprocate by switching roles and helping your partner at the end of your session.

Summary

1. Make statement about yourself.
2. Partner evaluates statement.
3. Partner redirects negative to positive.
4. Write down useful positive statements for reference.

Recording Results

Using the following headings, write in your notebook any positive statements that you feel comfortable with. Carry this list with you at all times for easy reference while you are building your new, positive habit.

Date	Situation	Positive Statement
4/16	Missed par	I'll correct it on the next hole.

Evaluating Progress

Whenever you have time, look at each statement closely. When practicing, always be aware of what you say to and about yourself.

As you make progress, positive statements become second nature, with negative statements disappearing from your thoughts.

Changing Behavior During Team Competition

Help yourself and your playing partners eliminate negative behavior. **Assist each other in identifying negative behaviors and replacing them with positive behaviors.**

Your partners must agree 100% with the following game plan.

1. Any time a partner is observed acting in a negative, self-defeating manner, any other partner may stop and redirect him or her into positive behavior.
2. The redirected partner must identify what positive behavior would be more beneficial in a similar situation, write it down, and resolve to use the positive, replacement behavior the next time such a situation occurs.
3. **Optional:** To reinforce positive behavior and foster good spirit, have the offending partner contribute some money to the "kitty" each time a he or she is identified as saying or doing something that represents a negative self thought or behavior. Use the money at the end of the season to have a party or as a prize for the "most improved attitude."

Summary

1. Playing partners redirect each other during competition.
2. Offender identifies and writes down offending behavior, and resolves to use positive behavior.
3. Partners reinforce each others' positive behavior.

Recording Results

Using the following headings, write in your notebook the positive, replacement behavior you will use the next time a similar situation occurs during competition. Carry this list with you at all times for easy reference while you are building your new, positive habit.

Date	Situation	Positive Behavior
3/27	Hit ball carelessly.	I will concentrate on the next shot.

Evaluating Progress

Always before competition and whenever else you have time, look at your notes on each situation and positive behavior closely. When competing, always be aware of how you act.

 As you make progress, positive behaviors become second nature to you and your playing partners, with negative behaviors disappearing from your group's repertoire.

4 You Can Use the Super Powers of Your Mind!

When you accept the notion that whatever the mind believes, the body believes, you already have an enormous competitive edge. As you learn how to control what your mind believes, your ability to perform at maximum potential increases dramatically! The amazing thing is that you can use the power of your mind at home and on the golf course to improve the quality and consistency of your shot.

Visualizing Your Way to Success

The following sections describe the concept of visualization (mental practice or mental rehearsal). See **Mental Practice Drills** for detailed directions.

The Power of Mental Practice (Visualization)

Visualization is a classic example of focused imagination. Another name for it is mental imagery, or just imagery. If you imagine yourself practicing a skill, it is called mental practice. Every bit of it is as simple as ABC. Here is how it works with golf.

To practice your shot, just close your eyes and imagine that you are setting up on the tee, fairway, or green, executing your shot perfectly, and sending the ball to the desired destination. As a bonus, you can focus your imagination — just like a microscope — on any kind of situation you desire. If you are having trouble driving, imagine driving. If you are having trouble with a particular shot, set it up in your mind and "see" yourself executing the shot perfectly.

> **Example:** Mental practice is very effective and worthwhile. A research project conducted with basketball free-throw shooting provides the perfect example. Youngsters of equal ability were divided into three groups. Group 1 practiced free throws every day. Group 2 did nothing but use their imaginations to visualize perfect free-throw shooting every day. Group 3 did both.
>
> As you might guess, Group 3, the group that practiced both physically and mentally, did the best in the final test. But what surprises most people is that there were no significant differences between the group that only practiced physically and the group that only practiced mentally. Both groups significantly increased their free-throw shooting ability compared to their skill levels before testing. Visualized practice produced the same results in free-throw effectiveness as actual physical practice.

Obviously, real physical practice is necessary to develop the basic muscular skills. But this research demonstrates that correct visually-imagined practice does help to refine learned physical skills.

The best way to develop mental imagery skills quickly is to visualize both at home and at the course. As you develop the basics at home you will develop skill in visualizing the act of executing shots on the course.

Mental Practice at Home

You don't have to be at the golf course to improve your game. If you set aside at least 15 minutes for visualization, or success imaging, and practice faithfully, each day, for 8 days, you will see significant benefits in real situations.

You can use a regulation scorecard or draw up a scorecard. Sit in a comfortable chair in a quiet room and relax. You will check off the holes as your mental practice round progresses. You can visualize making drives, approach shots, chips, and putts, as well as coping with problem course conditions and other difficult situations.

The list of situations in which you can visualize success is as long as you desire. The idea is to always see yourself dealing with them perfectly, in detail.

Golfing Tough in Clutch and Disturbing Situations

When you know how to use mental practice, you can create clutch or otherwise disturbing golfing situations in your mind and visualize yourself playing successfully during these situations — in other words, Golfing Tough. Such elements may be noise, other people playing next to you, high-stress tournament competition, etc. First, you must identify specific high-pressure situations. Then, you can carry out the sequence, as shown, below.

Mental Practice for **Golfing Tough**

Remember, your body believes what you tell it to believe. If you create a success history in your mind, that is what the body will react to, not the potential for failure. Your ability to perform up to your physical ability in real situations will increase!

 Tell your body that you can play successfully in both clutch and disturbing situations. It works! Take charge.

Combining Mental Practice with Physical Practice

You can put success imaging into real situations by combining mental practice with physical practice exactly as described below. By hitting at least 60 practice shots each day for 8 consecutive days, you help to "lock in" the association between visualization of your form and execution of each shot. You will soon find that the visualization process takes an extremely small amount of time. In fact, regular golfing partners may not even be aware of your new technique.

 Focus only on what is within your control — a high-quality shot.

Mental Practice During Competition

The success imaging process is useful right on the course during competition. Again, no one will know what you are doing. It's easy when you know how. As you wait for your turn, simply close your eyes for a few seconds and visualize an absolutely correct and successful shot, with perfect execution of your shot.

Your body takes this mental image of precision and success with it into the setup as you prepare your shot. You must do this before every shot — before attempting swings, chips, and putts, no matter how easy or difficult!

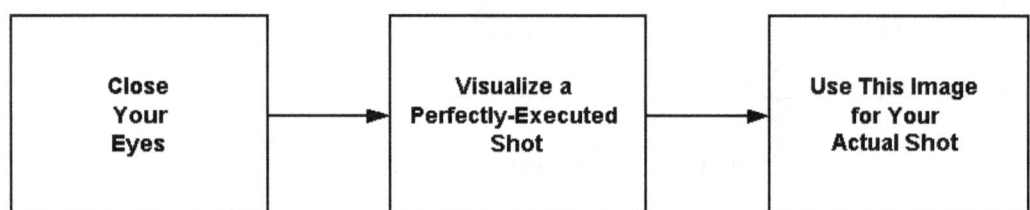

Mental Practice During Competition

In the chapter titled 6 You Can Make Mental Toughness Routine!, you are given some additional preparation and organizing skills that make your consistent use of mental practice during competition much easier.

 Visualizing success puts the odds in your favor, because you keep your mind focused on execution only and off of making birdies and eagles, or winning.

Visualizing with Video

Today, you can use video to see yourself instantly, anywhere — at home or in the clubhouse. You can help to refine and ingrain your shot by watching a video recording of an ideal shot.

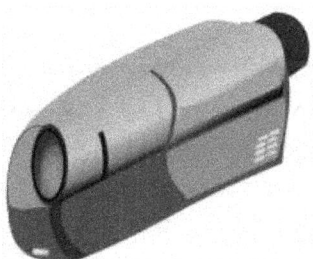

When you are performing well, video record yourself and keep it for reference and review. It is helpful to watch yourself executing consistently well. If you are not performing well, you may watch a performance of someone else with form similar to the form you desire to have. Do not watch someone who swings vastly different. For example, if you are a golfer with a long, free swing, it could corrupt your shot to watch a herky-jerky golfer with a short, fast swing!

Watch the appropriate performance every day for 8 consecutive days, playing as soon as possible after each viewing. A variation of this technique is to take the video player to the course and watch yourself immediately before making a shot.

Endless Possibilities with Super Mind Power

As you can see, the power of your mind is awesome. Whatever your mind believes, your body will react to faithfully. You can have the competitive edge you desire by putting beneficial information into your mind. To do this, you must be selective.

Now you know how to use visualization to program your body movements at home or at the golf course, in practice or in competition. You can effectively visualize yourself making birdie or par shots in all types of normal, clutch, and otherwise troublesome situations. You can be successful with mental imagery, all you must do is practice, practice, practice.

 Everyone uses imaging. Those who imagine failure will probably fail. Those who imagine success will have a greater chance to succeed.

Mental Practice Drills

For the drills on the following pages, keep a notebook so you can see your total progress. Label a page or section with the name of the drill at the top. Your notes are private, so keep them in your bag between shots.

Mental Practice at Home or When Alone

Increase your ability to use mental practice (visualization) on a consistent basis to improve and maintain a high level of physical performance, by practicing at home. Play at least two visualized rounds per day. Never visualize missing your goal; there is no payoff for visualizing disaster except to create real disasters.

Directions

1. Get a regulation scorecard or draw up a scorecard on a sheet of paper.
2. Find a quiet place to relax and sit in a comfortable chair, but do not lie down during this drill because you need to make notes. You will check off the holes as your mental practice round progresses.
3. Use the relaxation session to get yourself in a receptive state of mind before you start.
4. Do the following drills, trying to make your visual image as real as possible; with all of the sights, sounds, smells, and other sensations normally associated with a real golf setting.
   - **Drives:** On each shot, close your eyes and imagine that you are setting up and executing your drive perfectly, sending your ball as far as good execution allows straight down the fairway. Take your time! Visualize your absolutely correct, perfectly timed shot in detail. Do not visualize anything other than perfection.
   - **Fairway Shots:** On each approach shot, close your eyes and imagine that you are setting up and executing your shot perfectly, sending your ball to exactly the place you desire, whether it be simply closer to or on the green. Take your time! Visualize your absolutely correct, perfectly timed shot in detail. Do not visualize anything other than perfection.
   - **Chips:** On each chip shot, close your eyes and imagine that you are setting up and executing your shot perfectly, sending your ball at the appropriate speed toward he cup. Take your time! Visualize your absolutely correct and successful shot in detail. Do not visualize leaving anything other than perfection.
   - **Putts:** On each putt, close your eyes and imagine that you are setting up carefully on line and executing your shot perfectly, sending your ball to die in the center of

the cup. Take your time! Visualize your absolutely correct and successful shot in detail.
- **Course Conditions:** If you are having problems with particular course conditions, imagine yourself playing on and mastering such conditions. Visualize in detail as before, making appropriate adjustments to fit the conditions. Always visualize a successful outcome. Be sure that you know what to do in each situation; you should not visualize an incorrect solution to a given problem!

Summary

1. Relax your mind and body.
2. Visualize perfection.
3. Record results.
4. Evaluate your progress daily.

Recording Results

Use a regulation scorecard to record your score. Using the following headings in your notebook; make notes on the quality of your visualization for each and every shot.

Date	Hole #/Shot #	How Much Detail I Saw	How Thorough the Scene Was	How Crisp the Image Was
6/16	3/2	6	4	7

Evaluating Progress

Rate the characteristic above on a scale of 1 (worst or least) through 10 (best or most). Look for higher ratings over a period of 3 to 8 days.

You Can Use the Super Powers of Your Mind!

Mental Practice for Clutch and Disturbing Situations (Golfing Tough)

You can add specific negative elements to your mental environment and imagine yourself — in detail — playing golf successfully under clutch and disturbing conditions. Use the following steps to identify real clutch and disturbing situations. You will use such situations while coping to reduce tension.

The situations presented in the table below are for illustration only; they may not be appropriate to your personal situation. They are fairly typical and are given to help you develop your own.

Typical Disturbing Situations

Associated with:	Type of Disturbance
Specators	Audible conversation while you are setting up for a shot
	Excessive demand for your personal attention
	Yelling from a distance while you are setting up for a shot
	Past history of poor interaction with a specific individual
	Moving while in line of sight of golfer making a shot
	Presence of a significant individual in a crowd
Other Golfer	Audible conversation with caddie while you are making a shot
	Walking over the projected path of your ball on the green
	Moving while in your line of sight while you are making a shot
	Making unusual or inappropriate mannerisms
	Standing out of sight but in a hazardous location
	Making an inappropriate comment to you at any time
	Causing an unnecessary break in routine
	Past history of poor interaction with a specific individual
Internal	Lack of success in setting up for a difficult shot
	Recent history of poor timing or technique
	Stiffness or tension not caused by a physical injury
	Inability to overcome challenges of the course
	Inadequate preparation for intense competition
	Placing blame on previously effective equipment
	Becoming excessively angry with a bad break

Typical Disturbing Situations

Associated with:	Type of Disturbance
Past Failures	Losing focus during a tournament
	Losing a lead during the last few holes of a tournament
	Selecting the wrong club for a particular shot
	Misreading putts in similar situations

Summary for All Situations

1. Identify several high-pressure situations. Be specific.
2. Imagine yourself in the situation.
3. Visualize yourself executing calmly and perfectly.

Directions for Clutch Situations

1. In the spaces below, write a list of specific clutch golfing situations that are real to you.

> Example: Typical clutch situations may be, "I need this birdie to win the tournament." "I must get the ball within 50 yards of the green.", or "I must chip within five feet of the cup." Think back to the conditions that produced high tension when you were in the clutch.

a.

b.

c.

d.

e.
_____
_____
_____

2. Now, visualize yourself in detail, golfing in these situations. Focus only on making a perfect shot. Repeat visualization of a successful outcome at least 10 times a day for 8 consecutive days.

Directions for Disturbing Situations

1. In the space below, write a list of specific, disturbing golfing situations. These should be real to you and affect you negatively in some way.

> **Example:** A typical situation may be, "I do not like to play with Joe, he disturbs my concentration." Another may be, "I do not play well on this course." An off-course example may be, "I do not like the people at the Chopworm Golf Club, they bother me."

a.
_____
_____
_____

b.
_____
_____
_____

c.
_____
_____
_____

d.
_____
_____
_____

e.
_____
_____
_____

2. Now, visualize yourself in detail, golfing in these situations. Focus only on making a perfect shot. Repeat your visualization of a successful outcome at least 10 times each day for 8 consecutive days.

Recording Results for All Situations

Use a regulation scorecard to record your score. Using the following headings in your notebook; make notes on the quality of your visualization for each and every shot.

Date	Hole #/Shot #	How Much Detail I Saw	How Thorough the Scene Was	How Crisp the Image Was
7/11	6/2	7	5	4

Evaluating Progress for All Situations

Rate the characteristic above on a scale of 1 (worst or least) through 10 (best or most). Look for higher ratings over a period of 3 to 8 days.

Mental Practice During Solo Physical Practice

You can put success imaging into real situations by combining mental practice (visualization) with physical practice. Then, you can make mental practice a part of your overall Mental Toughness Routine (MTR) in practice. See **Taking Control of Your Mental Environment**.

Directions

1. Make sure that you are lined up properly for each shot and are executing correctly.
2. Then, play at least one round, visualizing a perfect result before each shot, as described in the exercise, Mental Practice at Home or When Alone, and summarized below. See yourself:
   - **Drives:** Setting up and executing your drive perfectly, sending your ball as far as good execution allows straight down the fairway.
   - **Fairway Shots:** Setting up and executing your shot perfectly, sending your ball to exactly the place you desire, whether it be simply closer to or on the green.
   - **Chips:** Setting up and executing your shot perfectly, sending your ball at the appropriate speed toward he cup.
   - **Putts:** Setting up carefully on line and executing your shot perfectly, sending your ball to die in the center of the cup.
   - **Course Conditions:** Mastering difficult conditions, making appropriate adjustments to fit the conditions. (Be sure to know what to do!)

Summary
1. Relax your mind and body.
2. Visualize perfect setup, execution, and results.
3. Make a well-executed shot.
4. Record results.
5. Evaluate your progress daily.

Recording Results

Use a regulation scorecard to record your score. Using the following headings in your notebook; making notes on the quality of your visualization for each and every shot.

Date	Hole #/Shot #	How Much Detail I Saw	How Thorough the Scene Was	How Crisp the Image Was
11/24	8/1	7	7	6

Evaluating Progress

Rate the characteristic above on a scale of 1 (worst or least) through 10 (best or most). As the quality of your visualization increases, you will become more accurate and consistent. Look for improvement over a period of 3 to 8 days of serious application.

Mental Practice During Competition

Use mental practice (visualization) consistently before each shot during competition to improve and maintain a high level of physical performance. Incorporate this habit of visualization into your Mental Toughness Routine (MTR) during competition.

Directions
1. Make sure that you are lined up properly for each shot and are executing correctly.
2. Then, begin taking about 3 to 5 seconds before each shot to visualize, in detail, the perfect shot. Always picture yourself as being successful before you make your shot. **Do not watch anyone else swing!** See yourself:
   - **Drives:** Setting up and executing your drive perfectly, sending your ball as far as good execution allows straight down the fairway.
   - **Fairway Shots:** Setting up and executing your shot perfectly, sending your ball to exactly the place you desire, whether it be simply closer to or on the green.

- **Chips:** Setting up and executing your shot perfectly, sending your ball at the appropriate speed toward he cup.
- **Putts:** Setting up carefully on line and executing your shot perfectly, sending your ball to die in the center of the cup.
- **Course Conditions:** Mastering difficult conditions, making appropriate adjustments to fit the conditions. (Be sure to know what to do!)

Summary

1. Relax your mind and body.
2. Visualize perfect setup, execution, and result.
3. Make a well-executed shot.
4. Analyze the shot and identify the element for improvement.
5. Write the element down and improve it on your next shot.

Recording Results

Keep your score on a regulation scorecard. After you finish a hole, using the following headings in your notebook, write out which element needs correction and improvement on the next shot.

Date	Hole #/Shot #	Element Needing Correction
4/14	9/2	*Alignment*

Do not slow down the pace of competition for the other players; keep your recording activity short and to the point.

Evaluating Progress

As the quality of your visualization increases, you will become more accurate and consistent. Look for improvement over a period of 3 to 8 days of serious application.

5 You Can Relax, Anywhere, Anytime!

Believe it or not, relaxation is not "normal." Regardless of what people may think, they are almost never completely relaxed. Total relaxation while sitting in a chair may result in your sliding to the floor. Total relaxation while standing results in total collapse. Conversely, total tension results in not being able to move even your little finger.

To perform at your best during competition, you need the useful balance between relaxation and tension that you are accustomed to during your maximum-performance practice sessions. Most golfers perform much better in practice because the stress of competition upsets the balance between relaxation and tension in favor of increased tension. How can you make yourself perform better during competition? Let's think about two different ways. You could (1) practice under tense conditions or (2) compete under relaxed conditions.

Using Willful Relaxation

The following sections describe the concept of willful relaxation. See the "Relaxation Drills" section for detailed directions.

Practicing Under Tense Conditions

Practicing under tense conditions is not an efficient use of your time. Practice is the quiet time during which you can learn how to relax mentally and make repeated physical movements in a mentally-relaxed state. A quiet, low-stress atmosphere for practice allows your muscles to make fine, consistent movements — and to learn them.

Just think of those times when you tried to practice while someone near you was talking loudly or when you, yourself, were laughing and talking with friends! These types of disruptions create non-productive and often tense practice conditions. Practice under such conditions disturbs your concentration and does not allow your physical movements to be as refined — efficient or accurate — as when playing relaxed.

You Can Relax, Anywhere, Anytime!

Competing Under Relaxed Conditions

It is best to learn how to relax during competition. If it is possible to perfect your shot under relaxed practice conditions, it only makes sense to mentally create the same conditions when you are in competition. You can learn how to make yourself relax during competition. As you develop this ability, you will discover that your relaxation-tension balance point is very close to what you experience during normal, noncompetitive practice situations.

Reaching Optimum Balance Between Relaxation and Tension

Few elements of nature work together with such consistency as the mind and body. Research tells us that, if the body's muscles are tense, then the mind is stressed. If the mind is stressed, then the muscles are tense. It is a vicious circle. Luckily for us, the opposite is also true. If the body is relaxed, the mind is relaxed and clear. If the mind is relaxed, the body is relaxed.

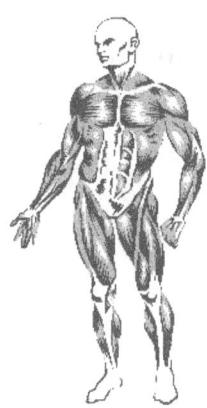

As you become more aware of bodily tension, you will discover that you have one particular muscle group (for example, jaw muscles, stomach muscles, forearm muscles, etc.) that tenses up before any other when you begin to react to stress. This sensitive muscle group, called a "threshold group", can serve as a trigger for your entire body. If it is tense, the rest of the body follows suit. However, when you can recognize the tension in that muscle group and relax it, the rest of the body will follow in a balanced manner.

Do not be concerned that you are learning to put yourself in an overly relaxed state. The natural tension that you feel when you really want to excel will not allow you to totally relax. The method you will learn in this book will not put you into a "deep" state of relaxation. It is designed to help you reach your own maximum balanced state between tension and relaxation that will allow you to perform at your peak physical level.

Recognizing and Relaxing Muscular Tension

The first step in learning to relax under stressful conditions is learning how to recognize muscular tension. The second step is learning how to replace excessive muscular tension with muscular relaxation. The key to achieving both lies in your mental awareness skills and your desire to change the state of your muscles.

To increase your awareness of the unbalanced muscular tension that places your ability to perform at risk, you have to first become aware of how tense you are under normal conditions. It is very difficult to recognize excessive muscular tension, because tension is a normal part of everyday life. Even many professional golfers never realize to what extent excessive muscular tension has eroded their ability to perform.

The most efficient way to learn how to recognize tension and to relax your muscles is by consciously alternating muscular tension and relaxation of the various muscle groups. At the end of the sessions, carried out exactly as described below, you will know clearly when you are under tension. You will be able to identify the primary muscle group and to actually relax those muscles when you want.

It really helps to listen to an audio relaxation session in which the speaker leads you in tensing and relaxing the various muscle groups.

> **You may make your own relaxation tape or CD, following the directions given in Appendix B, "Making a Relaxation Tape or CD", or you can obtain a professionally-made version. Several general relaxation narrative sessions are available for purchase. Most of these contain a 20-minute activity that helps you learn how to recognize muscular tension and reduce it on demand.**

Using the physical relaxation session, simply follow the directions in a quiet place where you can lie down and concentrate. After tensing each muscle group, always "let go" completely, returning to the beginning position and following the instructions to fully and completely relax that specific muscle group.

Participate by listening to the session 8 days in a row, each time trying to relax each muscle group more and more; taking it into an even deeper state of relaxation. Try to participate just before you practice and just before competition to acquire any real significant skill development in achieving muscular balance.

Using a Booster Tape or CD

It can be helpful to listen to a short-form, "booster" tape or CD of the relaxation session (about 5 to 10 minutes worth in your own voice) and a shortened coping session just before a major event. This booster is effective only after you have taken the regular eight-day program as explained above and are able to relax at will.

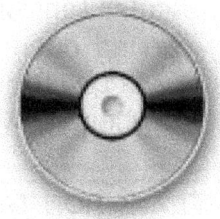

The objective is to focus only on your three most important (threshold) muscle groups that tense up the soonest or most often when presented with only the five most stress-producing situations with which you must cope. Think of it as an "express" way of calming down before performing.

See Appendix B Making a Relaxation Tape or CD for instructions on how to make your own, personal tape or CD.

 Practice relaxation all of the time — at home, at work, on the course, and before each and every shot in practice and tournaments! Put relaxation practice to good use whenever you feel stress or muscular tension growing

Relaxing in Real Golfing Situations

We have developed an additional way to increase your skills even faster and with more specific confidence (don't forget the power of the mind). It involves your using another session after the end of your relaxation sessions. This is called a "coping session", because

 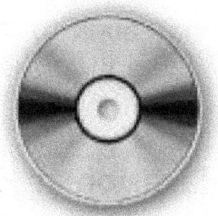

it assists you in coping with, or handling, difficult, real-life situations. This session presents to you a set of example situations specific to your golfing experience. You will add these, in your own voice, right on the tape or CD.

You can use the coping tape to extinguish your negative reactions to real and imagined clutch and disturbing situations that may have been causing anxiety and tension for a long time. You must use this coping strategy whenever you cannot calm yourself and play as relaxed as possible. Always use the coping strategy before competition and give yourself plenty of coping time before a tournament.

You must make this coping tape or CD session yourself; we cannot make it for you! Because you want to improve your ability to perform in real playing situations, the situations you pick to put on the tape or CD must reflect common playing situations for you. Thus, you can easily imagine that you are experiencing these situations because you actually have experienced them. **It is possible that you may not be aware of all things that bother you; therefore, it may be beneficial to identify these situations with the help of a sharp playing partner or caddie.** For the coping session to be effective, these situations must be presented to you in a specific sequence.

Therefore, if you will follow the steps given below, you will maximize your potential to achieve a balanced performance under stress conditions. You may use our examples if they apply to you, or you may create special ones for yourself with peoples' specific names. Also, keep in mind that as you extinguish your negative reactions to a selection of clutch or disturbing situations, others may surface that you must extinguish. However, there will be a time when very little will disturb your concentration. Look forward to that time!

See Appendix C Making a Coping Tape or CD for instructions on how to make your own, personal tape or CD.

You Can Relax, Anywhere, Anytime!

Relaxation Drills

For these drills, keep a notebook so you can see your total progress. Label a page or section with the name of the drill at the top. Your notes are private, so keep them in your bag between shots.

Practicing Willful Relaxation at Home

Be able to relax any muscle group on demand.

1. Anytime you are lounging around at home, pick one muscle group to practice tensing and relaxing (see Appendix B Making a Relaxation Tape or CD).
2. Tense and relax that single muscle group 10 times in a row.
3. Repeat this drill with at least 3 different muscle groups daily for at least 8 days.

    To provide variety, have your spouse or a friend surprise you 3 times a day with a verbal request for you to relax a certain muscle group. For example, a friend may turn to you while you are watching television and say, "Left forearm — NOW!" You then have 5 seconds to completely relax your left forearm. With this type of assistance, your ability to relax spontaneously will improve over time.

Summary

1. Tense and relax 3 different muscle groups daily for at least 8 days.
2. Record your results.
3. Evaluate your progress daily after 3 days.

    Optional: Relax on demand cue by spouse or friend.

Recording Results

Using the following headings, make daily entries in your notebook.

Date	Muscle Group	Relaxation Success
4/4	*Shoulder blades*	9

Evaluating Progress

Rate your "Relaxation Success", your ability to relax upon demand, on a scale of 1 (least) to 10 (most). After 3 days, look closely at your notes to see how well you are doing. Your ability to relax upon demand will increase significantly within 3 to 5 days and continue to improve with serious application. Each day, check to see what muscle groups need more work and focus on those during your next session.

Practicing Relaxation During Solo Physical Practice

Use this drill to increase your ability to relax and recover concentration and control during and after a distraction. **This drill makes you aware of your state of tension, as you see it.**

1. Practice swinging, making sure that you are lined up properly for each shot and that you are executing correctly.
2. Then, make at least 60 shots.
3. **Distractions:** Ask your friends to interrupt your concentration at least 10 times without warning during this session. They may talk behind you, shout at you (do not disturb other golfers), walk up next to you while you are addressing the ball, etc. However, they may not touch you or bring harm to anyone.

Summary

1. Execute 60 shots as well as you can.
2. Relax and recover your concentration quickly when disturbed.
3. Record results.
4. Evaluate your progress.

Recording Results

Keep a numerical score on a regulation scorecard. Using the following headings, make daily entries in your notebook. As soon as you have finished a shot, record your results.

Date	Shot #	Type of Distraction	Execution Quality	Ability to Relax	Ability to Concentrate
10/6	16	Noise	6	4	2

Evaluating Progress

Rate your "Execution Quality", "Ability to Relax" and "Ability to Concentrate" on a scale of 1 (poorest) to 10 (best). After 3 days, look closely at your notes to see how well you are able to relax and recover under stress.

Practicing Relaxation During Supervised Physical Practice

Use this drill to increase your ability to relax and recover concentration and control during and after a distraction. **This drill makes you aware of your state of tension, as your observer sees it.**

1. To improve your ability to relax after a distraction, practice while being watched by an observer. Make sure that you are lined up properly for each shot and that you are executing correctly.

2. Then, make at least 60 shots while being watched by an observer.

3. **Distractions:** Ask your friends to interrupt your concentration at least 10 times without warning during this session. They may talk behind you, shout at you (do not disturb other golfers), walk up next to you while you are addressing the ball, etc. However, they may not touch you or bring harm to anyone.

Summary

1. Execute 60 shots as well as you can.
2. Relax and recover your concentration quickly when disturbed.
3. Have your observer record results.
4. Have your observer evaluate your progress.

Recording Results

Using the indicated headings in your notebook or on a separate piece of paper, do the following:

1. Write down your own shot-by-shot evaluation of your "cone of focus", i.e. how well you seem to be relaxing and concentrating, i.e. what you think you are doing while you are attempting to recover from distractions.

2. Have your observer write down a shot-by-shot evaluation of what he or she observes about your relaxing and concentration, i.e. what you are visibly doing while you are attempting to recover from distractions.

Signs the observer should look for include: (ability to relax) your grinding your jaw, squeezing a towel, jiggling your leg, tapping your fingers, etc.; (ability to concentrate) your looking around at the score or watching other golfers, talking unnecessarily, etc.

Date	Shot #	Type of Distraction	Execution Quality	Ability to Relax	Ability to Concentrate
8/7	43	*Someone called my name.*	8	5	7

Evaluating Progress

Have your observer record the "Type of Distraction", then have him or her rate "Execution Quality", "Ability to Relax" and "Ability to Concentrate" on a scale of 1 (poorest) to 10 (best). After 3 days, look closely at your notes to see how your evaluation compares with that of your observer. You may be quite surprised to discover what another person sees.

Using Willful Relaxation During Competition

Develop the ability to relax on demand, increasing your concentration and control in real tournament play or during staged competition. Until the skill of willful relaxation is "locked in", you will have to monitor yourself and make notes. **Do not slow down the pace of competition for the other players; keep your recording activity short and to the point.**

1. First, make sure that you are lined up properly for each shot and that you are executing correctly.

2. During tournament play, as you are walking to your next shot, evaluate the quality of your relaxation and concentration. Try to correct any errors on your very next similar shot — do not wait!

3. After you finish a shot, write down an honest evaluation of it. Do not allow yourself to be influenced by the outcome; uptight people sometimes get birdies, and relaxed, focused people do occasionally have bogies.

Summary

1. Relax your mind and body.
2. Make a well-executed shot.
3. Analyze and evaluate execution, relaxation, and concentration.
4. Write down your evaluation.

Recording Results

Using the following headings, make notes on your performance between shots in your notebook.

Date	Shot #	Execution Quality	Specific Error/ Correction	Ability to Relax	Ability to Concentrate
11/1	21	9	Narrowed stance	7	6

Evaluating Progress

Rate your "Execution Quality", "Ability to Relax" and "Ability to Concentrate" on a scale of 1 (poorest) to 10 (best). If you made any error in your shot, write it down under "Specific Error/Correction", along with your strategy for correcting it — e.g. "...missed trajectory to the inside — follow through on line...." Review your notes after each competitive session (as time allows).

6   You Can Make Mental Toughness Routine!

All golfers unconsciously develop patterns of thinking that they use as they set up for each shot and between shots. Many develop thinking habits that are not very productive. They usually arise from a non-conscious level but, regardless of their source, they do not foster superior performance.

 **For consistently good performance, you must consciously establish a set of productive thinking habits that allow you to execute and hit your shot at your peak performance potential every time.**

To get you on your way, we encourage you to try our Mental Toughness Routine, or MTR. It combines the mental skills we have shown you so far into an easily-learned sequence that you use before each shot. It is a proven approach to establishing a strong pattern of productive thinking. If you use this routine consistently, clutch situations will have minimal impact on your ability to perform. You will truly be Golfing Tough!

Taking Control of Your Mental Environment

The MTR helps you stay on task during performance. But, you must maintain control of your thoughts and actions at other times as well. To provide a good mental environment for the MTR to work effectively, do the following.

- **Prepare your mind before you arrive at the course.** Use your relaxation tape or CD, mental practice, and positive self-statements as a way of focusing your mind on what you are about to do.

    "Psyching up" is actually calming down while being alert to the task. Maintain this focused attitude for the entire time you are on the course. You may abandon this attitude after competition ends.

- **Be sure to have used your coping tape or CD to extinguish any negative reaction to disturbing thoughts and situations.** It is extremely important to start out with a clean emotional slate! Let nothing cause you anxiety; take charge.
- **During the round, talk only if absolutely necessary to maintain progress of the game.** This is not a way of "psyching out" others! In fact, it has nothing to do with others. It is simply a way to keep your mind in the game. For example, you may break your concentration to confer about the score or a particular tournament rule, but once the issue is resolved, resume concentrating on your game.
- **Do not watch anyone else swing while you are trying to program your mind for performance!** To do so will corrupt the image you have of yourself swinging. The only image you want in your mind is your own perfect performance. Although there is great similarity among the movement of elite golfers, seeing other golfers swing can interfere with the quality of your shot, both during competition and during mental and physical practice.
- **Between shots, keep others from talking to you unnecessarily by avoiding prolonged eye contact.** If you have to greet others, say "Hello", and shake hands, but do not engage in a long conversation.

Mental Toughness Routine

The Mental Toughness Routine (MTR) is an organized series of activities that you use to increase the quality and consistency of your shot.

The MTR helps you control only that over which you have direct control — execution of your shot. More consistently high scores and winning will follow.

The MTR works by keeping your mind focused on beneficial thoughts and actions while you are performing. At the same time, it keeps thoughts of failure out of your mind. As you get into the habit of using the MTR, it becomes much easier to use. It will not be automatic, however, so you must use it consciously all of the time — especially during tournaments.

Take a quick look at the Mental Toughness Routine Flowchart on the following page, paying special attention to the boxes, their headings, and the beneficial activities under each heading.

Each box represents a phase, or period of time. One phase flows into the next. Beneficial activities occur during each phase and are, themselves, arranged into rough time slots.

Beneficial activities may be mental or physical. Let's look a little closer at what happens during each phase.

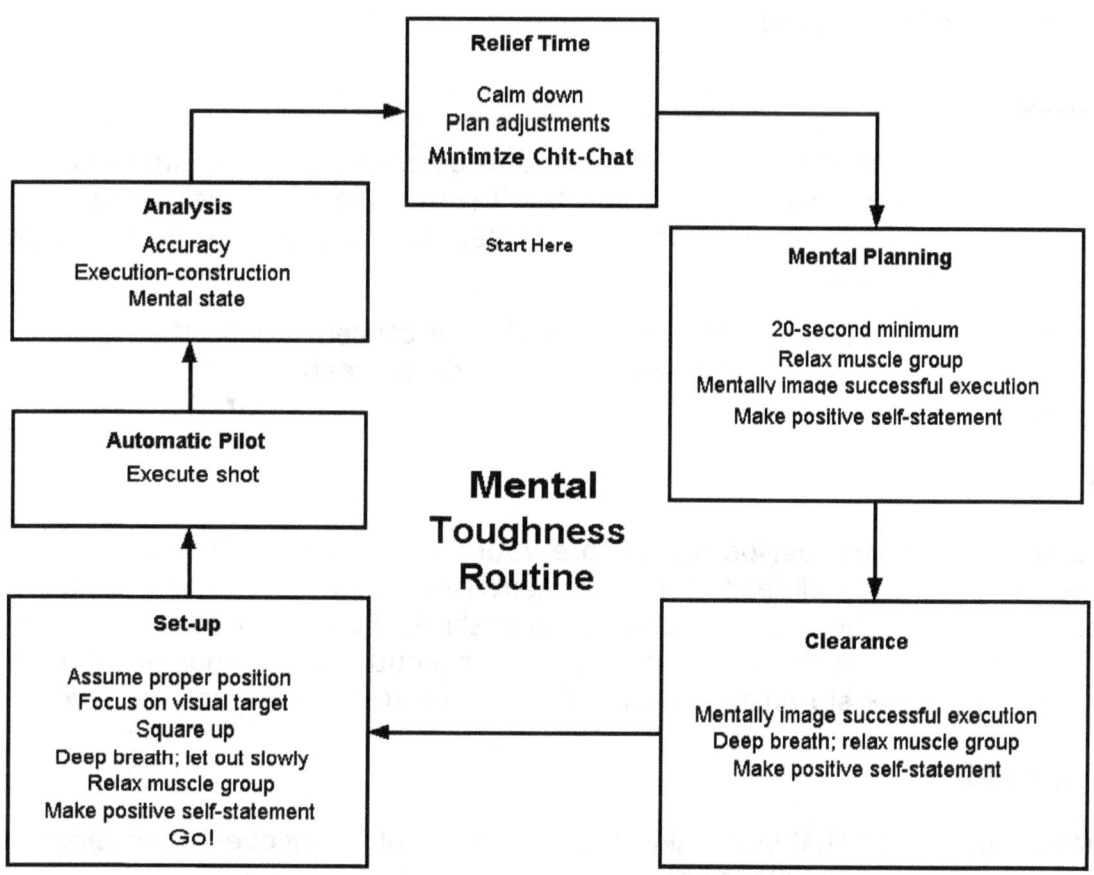

Relief Time

Relief Time begins just after your previous shot. It lasts during the time walking to where the next shot will take place. After completing a shot, be calm and plan the next shot. Although you do not need to begin focusing your attention on execution during this stage, it is still important to talk only when absolutely necessary. Remain calm and focused.

Mental Planning

Mental Planning begins after Relief Time. It is the time during which you begin a concentrated effort to focus your thoughts and apply your mental skills. As you learned earlier, you probably have a threshold muscle group that tenses up first when you are under pressure. Relax this muscle group. Then, imagine yourself successfully executing your next shot. Make a positive statement to yourself. Keep repeating your mental imagery and positive self-statements until it is your turn to swing again. Be aware of muscle tension and relax as needed.

Clearance

Clearance compares to the "batter up" period in baseball. It is the time when you are preparing to step up and begin your setup. Don't rush, take your time! Imagine yourself making a successful shot. Repeat this until it is clear in your mind. Although tempting at this point, do not watch anyone else swing.

Check to see if there is anything that may disturb your concentration. If all is clear, then, step up to where you will take your setup. Take a deep breath and make a positive self-statement. Then, step up into position.

Setup

Setup is the preparation period just before your shot during which you make sure that your body is lined up and ready for movement (see Chapter 1, "The Ultimate Clutch Solution: Your Mind"). Do not cut your setup time short. Focus your eyes on your ball and take a deep breath. Let the air slowly out of your mouth. Relax your threshold muscle group. Make a positive statement to yourself. When your mind is quiet, start your swing.

Automatic Pilot

Automatic Pilot means that you make your shot without being overly conscious of your movements. To do this with confidence, you must be well-practiced. Your physical movements should be so ingrained that your shot is reliable every time.

Analysis

Analysis is the time immediately following your shot. During this time, you must realize what was correct or incorrect with your shot. You may not have been lined up correctly. Your shot may not have "felt" right. Your mental state may not have been the best. At any rate, take time to analyze your previous shot. Also, do not start any conversation until <u>after</u> you have completed your analysis.

MTR Incorporation Drill

Use this drill during practice or during a staged competition to help you incorporate all of the habits you have learned from previous chapters into your Mental Toughness Routine (MTR) during competition.

During practice, carry a copy of the MTR in your pocket so you can refer to it quickly during your Relief and Mental Planning phases. Until a skill is "locked in", you will have to monitor your development in all competitive situations. **Do not slow down the pace of competition for the other players; keep your analysis and note-taking activity short and to the point.**

> When you are certain that you use all of the techniques consistently, you will not have to make notes. However, if you experience lapses in concentration and correcting errors, run this drill again, until you are performing effectively.

1. First, make sure that you are lined up properly for each shot and that you are executing correctly.
2. As you are walking to your ball, evaluate the quality of your relaxation, concentration, and execution.
3. After you finish a shot, make an honest evaluation of the previous shot. Do not allow yourself to be influenced by the outcome; uptight people sometimes get birdies, and relaxed, focused people do occasionally have bogies!
4. Plan and resolve the correction of any errors on your very next similar shot — do not wait!
5. Run all of the the MTR steps that precede your next shot, including relaxation, visualization of perfect execution, and positive self-talk.

Summary

1. Relax your mind and body.
2. Make a well-executed shot.
3. Analyze and evaluate relaxation and concentration.
4. Write down your evaluation if possible.
5. Plan and resolve how to correct errors.
6. Run MTR.

Recording Results

Using the following headings, make notes on your performance between shots in your notebook.

Date	Hole #/ Shot #	Ability to Relax	Ability to Visualize	Positive Self-talk	Ability to Analyze	Ability to Correct
12/12	7/1	7	9	6	4	5

Evaluating Progress

Rate the effectiveness of your "Ability to Relax", "Ability to Visualize", "Positive Self-talk", "Ability to Analyze", and "Ability to Correct" on a scale of 1 (poorest) to 10 (best). If you made any error in your shot, write it down in the "Ability to Correct" column, after your numerical rating. Review your notes after each competitive session (as time allows).

 As you incorporate the techniques into your MTR, your actions will become automatic, your execution will improve in all situations.

A Final Word

Good golfing is making your best shot and, if needed, correcting it immediately on your very next shot! Smart golfing involves correcting all of the time — keeping your head in the game. Golfing Tough is smart golfing under pressure!

To Golf Tough effectively all of the time, do the following consistently.

1. **Practice your physical game to know how your body should feel during a perfect shot.**

    No matter what your error, do not be critical of yourself — only constructive. Your objective is to think positively and productively so you can correct any errors on your very next shot.

2. **Collect your beneficial thoughts and actions into an organized Mental Toughness Routine and use this routine all of the time.**

3. **Stay focused on the only goal that is under your control — making one perfect shot.**

Golfing Tough is a privilege available to anyone. After finishing this book you now know enough to be as tough a golfer as your physical ability will allow you to be. Best of luck for future success!

 You can Golf Tough! Put what you have learned into practice every day and Golf Tough with the best!

You Can Make Mental Toughness Routine!

Appendix A Building a Reliable Physical Game

This section includes a list of instructional books to help you refine your physical golf game. Over the years, golf has had wonderful teachers, coaches, and performers that have attempted to share with readers what has been successful for them. Fortunately, unlike some other sports, golf instructors usually agree on a uniform set of techniques that have been successful for others. Therefore, the majority of modern golfers look similar when swinging a club. These books may make similar recommendaions, but the authors may state their case in different language. Also, some authors may have prioritized their recommendaions in a different order. However, regardless of the insight to be gained from these books, it is vital that you work with a good instructor to structure a reliable physical game. Then you will be able to apply the mental skills more effectively.

Classic Golf Instruction, (Brent Kelly, About Sports)

Ben Hogan's 5 Lessons: The Modern Fundamentals of Golf by Ben Hogan, Herbert Warren Wind, and artist Anthony Ravielli

Harvey Penick's Little Red Book by Harvey Penick

Bobby Jones on Golf by Bobby Jones

Swing the Clubhead by Ernest Jones

On Learning Golf by Percy Boomer

Golf My Way by Jack Nicklaus

The Gist of Golf by Harry Vardon

Search for the Perfect Swing by Alastair Cochran and John Stobbs

Practical Golf by John Jacobs

Sam Snead's Natural Golf by Sam Snead and Tom Shehan

Better Golf the Sam Snead Way by Sam Snead with Don Wade

Swing Easy, Hit Hard by Julius Boros

Modern Books

Dave Pelz's Short Game Bible by Dave Pelz and James A. Frank

Secrets of the Short Game by Phil Mickelson

Two Steps to a Perfect Golf Swing by Shawn Humphries

The Art of the Swing by Stan Utley

Swing Like a Pro by Dr. Ralph Mann and Fred Griffin

The Keys to the Effortless Golf Swing by Michael McTeigue

The Slot Swing by Jim McLean

The Eight-Step Swing, 3rd Edition by Jim McLean

The Golf Swing´s Simple Secret by J F Tamayo

Hank Haney's Essentials of the Swing by Hank Haney

The Picture-Perfect Golf Swing by Michael Breed

Tension-Free Golf by Dean Reinmuth

The Square-to-Square Golf Swing by Dick Aultman and artist Anthony Ravielli

Getting Up and Down by Tom Watson

The Timeless Swing by Tom Watson

Strategic Golf by Tom Watson

Appendix B Making a Relaxation Tape or CD

> **Note:** As an authorized purchaser of Playing Tough, you may download Dr. J. C. McCroskey's Relaxation audio in MP3 format from http://www.roberthstrickland.com/Relaxation/Relaxation.htm. (Case Sensitive) Click "Download the relaxation audio here." When prompted, type the User Name: "purchaser" and the Password: "authorized."

If you would like to make your own complete relaxation session or the shorter, more focused, booster session(s) on tape or CD, here are the directions.

Directions for Making a Relaxation Tape or CD

The physical relaxation session focuses on all of your muscles and several of your most stressful situations. On direction of the narrator (in this case, yourself) you are given the opportunity to learn how to tense and relax your muscies completely at will, in a quiet place where you can lie down and concentrate. We recommend that you listen to the relaxation session two times per use.

1. Get a tape recorder and a blank audio cassette tape with at least 30 minutes of recording time on a side. The reason is that you need to record two identical relaxation sessions on one side and leave ten minutes blank so you can record a coping session right after it, as described in Chapter 5. Alternatively, you can record directly onto a computer or digital recorder and copy the .wav or .mp3 file to a CD.
2. Find yourself a nice, quiet place to record.
3. Record the following introduction on only the first part of your tape or CD. Speak slowly.

    "Close your eyes, lie on your back and relax (the "beginning position"). Place your arms at your sides with the palms down. Look inward to sense the satisfying

feelings of true relaxation. Let your muscles go and search for the deep, deep pleasure of full relaxation.

(Pause for a while to give yourself time to reach full relaxation!)

Now, we are going to start a series of actions that involve alternating the tension and relaxation of specific muscle groups throughout your body. As you tense a muscle group do not try to produce extreme levels of tension; you may pull a muscle! Good solid tension will do the job — just enough so you can tell, without a doubt, that the muscle group is tense."

4. Record the following instructions for each muscle group (body part), using a higher, sharper tone of voice when you want to reflect tension and a lower, softer tone of voice when you want to reflect relaxation.

> Note: We use the muscle group of the left and right hands to illustrate the pattern for recording. When you are actually recording, substitute the muscle group and its accompanying tension instruction in the proper places indicated by parentheses, below.

"Start with your (left hand). (Make a fist) and increase the pressure. Hold it ... now, relax. Feel the muscles relaxing and the pleasant feelings as the muscles fall deeper and deeper into complete relaxation.

(Leave enough time to tense and relax and to feel complete relaxation!)

Try it again. Tense your (left hand), feel the muscles getting tense and rigid. Hold it ... now slowly relax the muscles. Feel the (left hand) getting loose and the muscles becoming free and lying back against the bones.

(Leave enough time to tense and relax and to feel complete relaxation!)

Now try your (right hand). (Make a fist) and increase the pressure. Hold it ... hold it ... now relax. Feel the muscles relaxing and the pleasant feelings as the muscles fall deeper and deeper into complete relaxation.

(Leave enough time to tense and relax and to feel complete relaxation!)

Try it again. Tense your (right fist), feel the muscles getting tense and rigid. Hold it .... now slowly relax the muscles. Feel the (right hand) getting loose and the muscles becoming free and lying back against the bones."

Continue, following the instructions, below.

Muscle Group	Tension Instructions
Left Hand	"Make a fist."
Right Hand	"Make a fist."
Back of Lt. Hand	"Tilt your hand backward at your wrist."
Back of Rt. Hand	"Tilt your hand backward at your wrist."
Left Biceps	"Press your left fist against your left shoulder."
Right Biceps	"Press your right fist against your right shoulder."
Left Foot	"Curl your left toes toward your heel, tighten your foot."
Right Foot	"Curl your right toes toward your heel, tighten your foot."
Left Calf	"Point your left toes away from your knee, tense your calf."
Right Calf	"Point your right toes away from your knee, tense your calf."
Left Shin	"Bend your left foot upward toward your knee; make it tight."
Right Shin	"Bend your right foot upward toward your knee; make it tight."
Left Thigh	"Straighten your left leg; make your thigh muscles hard."
Right Thigh	"Straighten your right leg; make your thigh muscles hard."
Stomach	"Make your stomach hard, like a brick."
Chest	"Tense up your chest muscles, make them hard."
Shoulders	"Bring both your shoulders up to touch your ears."
Front of Neck	"Lift your head and press your chin into your chest."
Back of Neck	"Push your head back, press against the surface."
Tongue	"Press your tongue up against your roof of your mouth."
Eyes	"Squeeze your eyes shut and lower your eyebrows."
Forehead	"Wrinkle up your forehead."

5. Re-record the relaxation session once: It should take about 10 minutes to record the session, so go ahead and record it again on the second 10-minute portion of the tape or CD. This will make your two relaxation sessions about 20 minutes long.

6. **Listen to the sessions. After tensing each muscle group, always "let go" completely, returning to the beginning position and following the instructions to fully and completely relax that specific muscle group.** Give yourself sufficient time to return to the beginning position and to feel the complete relaxation; you will need approximately 10 seconds of quiet time.

7. Repeat the listening session 8 days in a row. Each time, try to relax each muscle group more and more, taking it into an even deeper state of relaxation.

Appendix C Making a Coping Tape or CD

If you will follow the steps given below in making your own, personal coping tape or CD, you will maximize your potential to achieve a balanced performance under actual stress conditions. You may use our examples if they apply to you, or you may create special ones for yourself with peoples' specific names. Here are the directions.

Directions for Making a Coping Tape or CD

1. Identify three low-stress golfing situations that do not cause you any undue stress or muscular tension. Put these situations into an "experiencing" sentence. Remember, these situations do not cause you stress; they are either pleasurable or neutral.

   > **Example:** "I am practicing with my best friend.", or "I am showing my young niece how to golf.", or "I am out golfing for fun with my friends."

   Write out your low-stress situations below. Place the most pleasurable one first and the neutral or least pleasurable one last.

   a. _____
   _____
   _____

   b. _____
   _____
   _____

   c. _____
   _____
   _____

2. Now, identify any three moderate-stress golfing situations that cause you a small to moderate level of stress or muscular tension. Using the same format, list these situations in the spaces below.

> **Example:** "I am on the green and just getting ready to putt for a birdie.", or "The first three team members have bogeyed and they are looking to me to start a string of birdies.", or "I'm golfing in a weekly tournament and everyone is watching to see if I get a birdie.", or "I am in a money tournament and getting ready to hit my first ball."

Remember to use situations that work for you. If you're a professional golfer, the situations that cause you moderate stress are different from those that cause moderate stress for a recreational golfer.

Write out your moderate stress situations. Place the least tension-producing one first and the most tension-producing one last.

d. _____
_____
_____

e. _____
_____
_____

f. _____
_____
_____

3. Finally, identify three high-stress golfing situations in which you experience high levels of stress or muscular tension. Use the same method as above.

> **Example:** "I have three birdies in a row and am about to drive the ball.", or "I have to have a birdie on this ball for the team to win.", or " My opponent has the first four birdies and I have only pared.", or "All of the money depends on sinking this shot, and my opponent keeps talking loudly and jingling a key chain."

4. Remember, these should be troublesome situations to you. The experiences should really "bother" you.

   Write out your high stress situations below. Place the least tension-producing one first and the most tension-producing one last.

   g. _____

   h. _____

   i. _____

5. Wind your relaxation tape forward to the end of the relaxation session or record into a computer and add the .wav or .mp3 file after the relaxation session on the CD. Record in your own voice the following introductory instructions at the start of the coping session.

   "I am going to imagine myself in a series of golfing situations. As I mentally imagine the situation to be real, I will make every effort to recognize tension and relax the muscles in my body. When I recognize muscular tension, I will focus on that specific muscle group and enjoy relaxing it."

6. Then, record the situation statements you listed in a "low, moderate, high" sequence. Use a convincing voice and record them in the specific order shown below. Make a statement every 30 seconds; let there be complete silence until you make the next statement (that is, a 5-second statement, followed by approximately 25 seconds of silence). **This silent time is when you willfully relax your muscles in response to the situation!**

   A-B-C - B-C-D - C-D-E - D-E-F - E-F-G - F-G-H - G-H-I

   Statement A (low) is first, followed by statement B (moderate), then by statement C (high). Then drop statement A and repeat statements B and C, adding statement D (low). Then drop statement B and repeat statements C and D, adding statement E (moderate). Repeat this pattern until you have recorded all of your statements.

   Be sure to leave silence after each situation statement.

7. In the peace and quiet of your home, select a place where you can lie down (bed, sofa, recliner, etc.) and where you will not be interrupted by anyone.

8. Turn on the sessions at a comfortable volume, listen to the relaxation and coping sessions, doing exactly what you are told to do. Imagine yourself in each real coping situation. **Stay awake! If you fall asleep, you will have to start the session all over again!**

    Each time you hear a coping statement, pay attention to how your body reacts to it. Focus on relaxing any muscles that become tense as a reaction to the statement. Deliberately and consciously relax the reactive muscle group or groups during the silence that follows each statement.

9. **Listen to the relaxation and coping sessions each day for 8 consecutive days. At the end of that time, you will be able to recognize tension and reduce it whenever you want and in response to real situations. You will consciously relax under pressure! You will be in control!**

Directions for Making a Booster (Relaxation/Coping) Tape or CD

The "booster" tape or CD is a short-form version of the full relaxation session; it runs for only about 5 to 10 minutes, in your own voice. A shortened coping session is placed after the relaxation session (see *14 Making a Relaxation Tape or CD*). Use it just before a major event. This booster is effective only after you have taken the regular eight-day program as explained above and are able to relax at will. It focuses on only your three most important (threshold) muscle groups and five most stress-producing situations.

1. **Relaxation Session:** Follow the same pattern as the long version described above. However, do not record the introduction, and record a session that deals with only your three threshold muscle groups. Record it only once.

2. **Coping Session:** Add a session dealing with only the five situation statements you listed that give you the greatest amount of stress. Make a statement every 30 seconds, leaving approximately 25 seconds of silence after each statement to feel and reduce tension. Because there are only five statements made three-at-a-time, the specific order is:

    E-F-G - F-G-H - G-H-I - H-I

    Listen to the situation statements. Pay close attention to see which muscles react by becoming tense. Then, deliberately and consciously relax the reactive muscle group or groups during the silence that follows each statement.

Index

A

analysis 74
anger
   productivity 18
anxiety
   nervousness 19
   obstacle to a smooth swing 20
   part of competition 24
anxious 24
audiotape
   relaxation 63
automatic pilot 74

B

behavior
   changing on team 43
   negative 36
booster CD 64

C

CD
   booster 64
   relaxation 63
clutch situation
   examples 15
   how it develops 13, 15
   impact on performance 19
   personal 16
   pressure 13
   professional golfers 14
   stress 13
coach
   ongoing relationship 21
competition
   mental practice 50, 58
   relaxation during 66
coping 65
   CD 85
   tape 85

correcting
   smart golfing 77
course conditions
   mental practice 53, 57, 59

D

decisions
   conscious 32
   non-conscious 23
drills
   mental practice 52
   relaxation 66
   self-talk 42

E

emotions
   negative 18
   out of control 18

F

failure
   belief that you will fail 27
   event production 36
   fearing 25
   potential 14
focus
   detraction by behavior 36
   mental toughness routine 72
frustration
   factors beyond your control 37, 38, 39
   release by behavior 37

G

goal
   unreasonable 16
golfing situations
   high-stress 86
   moderate-stress 86
golfing smart
   correcting 77
Golfing Tough 13

H

help
  jointly, by playing partners 39
herky-jerky swing 51

I

instructor
  ongoing relationship 21

K

keyed up 29

M

mattering
  non-belief 28
mental planning 73
mental practice
  at home 49, 52
  course conditions 53, 57, 59
  drills for improvement 52
  during competition 50, 58
  during physical practice 57
  on the course 50
mental toughness routine
  focus 72
  MTR 71
mind power 51
movements
  trusting 21
MTR
  mental toughness routine 71
  phases 72
muscle tension
  stress 62
muscular tension
  recognizing 63

N

negatives
  effects of thought 14
  eliminating 38
  recognizing 37, 40, 41
  replacing with positives 38, 41

O

odds
  knowing 25
on-course situation
  visualization 56

P

performance
  impact of clutch situations 19
performance system
  incorporating behaviors 32
phases of MTR 72
practice
  mental skills 31
  partner-recorded results 43
  physical game only 31
  solo and self-talk 43
  tense conditions 61
programming
  talking to your brain 35

R

relaxation
  attaining a deeper state 84
  audiotape 63
  balance with tension 61
  CD 63
  drills for improvement 66
  during competition 66
  during solo practice 66
  not normal 61
  practice at home 66
  real situations 65
relief time 73

S

self-talk
  at home 42
  drills for improvement 42
  during solo practice 43
  partner intervention 43

setup 74
shot
   mechanically poor 31
   mental practice 47
   tips for reliability 79
shot clearance 74
shots
   mental practice drill 52, 57, 58
skilled golfer
   vs tough golfer 93
stress
   clutch situation 13
   competition 61
   high level and performance 18
   immunity 24
   muscle tension 62
   overcoming with mental skills 25
   overpowering 29
   part of competition 24
   performance 65, 85
   personal 15
   recovery from 67
   relaxing 63
stressed-out 24
success
   fearing 26

T

talking to others
   effects 36
team behavior changing 43
tensing up
   trying harder 29
tension
   balance with relaxation 61
thinking
   positive 35
   productive 71
threshold muscle groups 64, 88
tough golfer
   vs skilled golfer 93
trying harder

   tensing up 29

V

video
   visualization 51
visualization
   mental practice 47
   on-course situation 56
   video 51

W

watching other golfers 72

Golfing Tough is successfully meeting the mental challenge of performing well, regardless of the level of competition or the amount of pressure. The difference between a skilled golfer and a tough golfer is that the tough golfer applies the appropriate mental toughness skills consistently! This is a privilege available to anyone.

After finishing this book you will know enough to be as tough a golfer as your physical ability allows. If you seriously and consistently apply the lessons described, you will incorporate the behaviors into your performance system that make sense to you, that fit your personality, and allow you to reach your goals.

You can:

Build Self-confidence!
- Increase your confidence through what you say to yourself and others.
- Establish the correct frame of mind for success.
- Act like a success.

Use the Super Powers of Your Mind!
- Visualize successful performance.
- Practice anytime, anywhere.
- Focus your mind for consistent, successful performance.

Relax, Anywhere, Anytime!
- Relax physically and mentally.
- Set and achieve realistic goals for yourself.
- Increase your knowledge of yourself and how you really feel about and react to real situations.

Make Mental Toughness Routine!
- Organize your thoughts and actions for consistent, high-level performance in practice and in tournaments.
- Apply useful knowledge and practice, practice, practice!

Will Powers, Ph.D., is retired Professor Emeritus of Communication Studies at Texas Christian University in Fort Worth, Texas. He has published over 150 books, articles and papers while conducting clinics and training programs around the world. Together with his wife, Lois, he has established a highly-successful management and career development consulting business showcasing the Tip-A-Day concept, a daily approach to developing enhanced communication skills.

For the past 18 years, Will has been helping people in the workforce perform at quality levels while under pressure (including executives, managers, speakers and athletes of all types). This book is an effort to bring those years of experience and specialized knowledge to the golfing industry on a national level.

Will and Lois studied physical performance skills under Bob Strickland.

Bob Strickland, M.S. has been bowling since 1958 and was a PBA member 1978 - 1993. He is the author of four bowling books — Perceptive Bowling, Bowling: Steps to Success, Teaching Bowling: Steps to Success, and Dynamic Customization. He has averaged over 200 since 1964, and his personal highs include a sanctioned 300/812, and an unsanctioned 300/847. In 1966, he was voted on the Dallas, Texas All-City team. In 1967, he was awarded an NDEA Title IV fellowship to pursue graduate study in science and education at the University of Georgia. Since then, he has successfully applied his scientific knowledge and educational training to bowling and other technical disciplines in his own, unique way. In 2000, Bob was voted into the Dallas Bowling Association Hall of Fame.

Bob was a regular contributor to the Bowlers Journal's informative "Pro Shop Forum", and wrote a syndicated instructional column, "Perceptive Bowling Tips". He also wrote regular features for Pro Shop Today, the newspaper of the International Bowling Pro Shop and Instructors Association and for Bowling Industry magazine. He is a student of skill acquisition for a variety of sports and studied biomechanics and kinesiology at TWU in Denton, Texas.

In 1989 and 1990, Bob and his wife, Sue, conducted clinics in Europe and Scandinavian countries, including Norway, Finland, Italy, England, Germany, Belgium and Holland. They also toured Korea, Japan, and Hawaii. Many of these clinics were interpreted into the native languages. Bob returned in 1991 to conduct a whirlwind tour of Sweden, Ireland, and Germany, and in 1993, Bob and Sue trained Swiss National Bowling Coaches in Stans, Switzerland. They both enjoy studying and playing golf.

Bob and Sue studied mental performance skills under Dr. Will Powers.

www.ingramcontent.com/pod-product-compliance
Lightning Source LLC
Chambersburg PA
CBHW080348170426
43194CB00014B/2722